Merciful Moments

A Devotional Journal
for Moving Forward With
Grace Each Day

KIRSTYN MAYDEN

Merciful Moments: A Devotional Journal for Moving Forward With Grace Each Day
Copyright © 2021 Kirstyn Mayden

Published & Designed by Milk & Honey Books, LLC
Cover Image: Creative-Family/Getty Images via Canva

This book is available at: www.milkandhoneybooks.com and other online retailers.
Reach us on the Internet: www.milkandhoneybooks.com

ISBN 13: 978-1-953000-12-5

For Worldwide Distribution, Printed in the United States of America
1 2 3 4 5 6 7 8 9 10

This Book Belongs to

Dedication

To John and Naomi:
Thank you for your amazing love and support of me. May our family continue to move forward receiving God's grace and mercy each day. For the reader who is needing a fresh wave of God's mercy, this devotional was written just for you.
Embrace God's merciful moments today!

Table of Contents

Introduction

We often hear the end of a person's testimony, and we celebrate how God moved mightily on their behalf, but we don't really know the entire story. We don't know the details of the past that they sought to overcome, and we don't know the private battles they may still be dealing with.

Thankfully, God's mercies are new every morning and there is always another opportunity to start again.

The steadfast love of the Lord never ceases, his mercies never come to an end; they are new every morning, great is your faithfulness.
(Lamentations 3:22-23 ESV)

Despite our imperfections, shortcomings, and not having it all together, every day God provides us with new grace, new mercies, and new strength to move forward.

Webster's Dictionary defines 'mercy' as "compassion or forbearance shown especially to an offender or to one who is subject to another person's power." The good news about God is that no mistake, failure, sin, or shame can separate us from His love and mercy. Still, we have to decide every day to receive it.

Moving forward with God's mercy is not always easy, but it is necessary if we want full, abundant, and grace-filled lives. God's grace is a free gift given to us out of His infinite kindness towards us, and combined with His mercy, provides us an opportunity to start again and move forward with a clean slate. God loves us just that much!

Merciful Moments: A Devotional Journal for Moving Forward With Grace Each Day is designed to encourage, empower, and sustain you with uplifting scripture and practical strategies and actions to help you move courageously forward in God's grace every day, with greater clarity.

Amidst life's ongoing challenges, disappointments, and seasons, how do we continue to walk in God's mercy each day? How do we maintain hope and vitality in our daily routines as we face life's challenges? When we don't "feel" God's presence, how do we maintain a heart of gratitude? As you read through each devotion, write down your thoughts, pray each suggested prayer, and begin to apply the practical strategies and action steps each chapter offers. You're invited to be renewed, refreshed, and reassured that God is with you and for you in every season of life.

Whether you're in a season of waiting, transition, frustration, or needing hope, *Merciful Moments* is your resource for real encouragement to help you keep the faith and receive the richness of God's mercy every day. From my personal experience, I know receiving God's mercy is not always easy, because it requires me to surrender control. The good news is that God knows the direction for our lives, is working on our behalf, and wants us to trust Him more and more.

I invite you to embrace God's restorative and revitalizing mercy and be confident that He is with you, He has your best interest in mind, and He has not forgotten about you. With each new day of God's mercy, don't lose hope. Keep moving forward in His grace.

Trust in the LORD with all your heart and lean not on your own understanding;
in all your ways submit to him, and he will make your paths straight.

Proverbs 3:5–6

Continue to Trust God

Trusting in God is easier when things are going well and life is in a good rhythm. Trusting God during change or uncertainty is much more difficult. Proverbs 3:5-6 instructs us to trust God with all of our heart. But what do we do when our heart is broken, confused, or hurting?
We trust anyway.

When I had my daughter and became a new stay-at-home mom, I did not know how I was going to navigate this new season and keep my sanity. I had more questions than answers and felt overwhelmed. While these feelings didn't immediately dissipate, God reminded me that He was ultimately in control. He reminded me that perfection isn't possible, and that I needed to continue to trust His guidance and provision. God also reminded me of the support He had placed around me.

Life is full of new seasons and unexpected changes. Trusting God is an action that takes practice and is developed with faith. Practice surrendering control over to God and resting in the knowledge that He understands and provides strength through the process. **Despite what season of life you are in, God is calling you to surrender and depend on Him more. It is in times of triumph and trial that trusting God is most necessary.**

In the natural world, we trust what we can see and what we can understand. But as we mature in Christ, God wants us to build our trust in Him when we cannot see and don't know what tomorrow brings. With God's new mercy, you can trust that He is walking with you each day and guiding you through the unknown, the uncomfortable, and even the scary new seasons in your life.

Prayer

Dear God, thank You for knowing what is best for my life. In times of uncertainty or difficulty, thank You for increasing my trust in You. At times when I want to know the outcome, may I surrender more to Your will.

In Jesus' name, amen.

Action

Write down what season of life you are in right now and what three areas you will trust and surrender to God in more.

Despite what season of life you are in, God is calling you to surrender and depend on Him more. It is in times of triumph and trial that trusting God is most necessary.

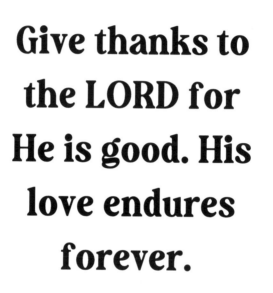

Give thanks to the LORD for He is good. His love endures forever.

Psalm 136:1

Give Thanks

Despite what season of transition you're in right now, give God thanks. There is always something to praise Him for in our lives. You can give thanks in a number of ways: write it in a gratitude journal, speak it out loud, sing about it in a song, or express it during a prayer walk among God's glorious outdoor creation. When my spirit needs encouragement, I pause and give thanks to God for His numerous blessings. Being grateful and expressing thanks to the Lord changes my perspective and reminds me that everything will be ok. If you can't find anything to be grateful for, look in the mirror. You are still here. God still has a purpose and assignment for you to accomplish, for His glory.

During seasons of life when you find it difficult to find peace, God will invigorate you by His Word. In the midst of doubt, anxiety, or weariness, it is easy to lose sight of our blessings or not take the time to pause. It's not easy to give thanks to God when we are frustrated, tired, or angry with Him. Still, when you feel depleted, that's the time I especially encourage you to give Him thanks, because it will refuel and re-strengthen your faith in Him to see you through. **Giving thanks to God is a powerful act of worship, to fortify you and remind you of His continual faithfulness.**

- Give thanks to God when your faith is wavering.
- Give thanks to God when you can't see your way forward.
- Give thanks to God to build up and comfort you during difficult seasons.
- Give thanks to God when you don't understand His ways or timing.
- Give thanks to God when you want to throw in the towel.
- Give thanks to God as a reminder of His unwavering love for you.

With each new day and God's mercy, give Him thanks.

Prayer

Dear God, thank You for Your abundant blessings in my life. At times when I am discouraged or can't "feel" Your presence, remind me of the importance of giving thanks to You as an act of reverence and of Your ongoing faithfulness. In Jesus' name, amen.

Action

Write a thank you letter to God. Name five to ten things, people, or situations you are grateful for today. Place it in an easily accessible place so that you can go to it for encouragement and as a regular reminder of God's faithfulness.

Giving thanks to God is a powerful act of worship, to fortify you and remind you of His continual faithfulness.

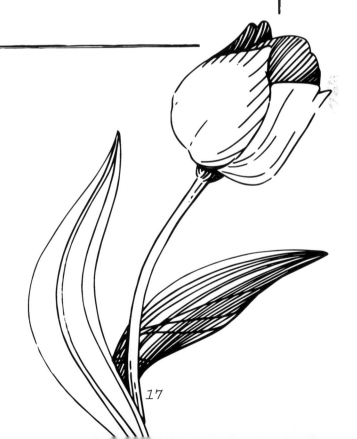

Two are better than one, because they have a good return for their labor: If either of them falls down, one can help the other up. But pity anyone who falls and has no one to help them up.

Ecclesiastes 4:9–10

Seek Community

God created us to be in community with one another. When I'm feeling down or needing encouragement, I always feel better when I spend time with family or friends. Sometimes, I just need a listening ear, a good laugh, or a delicious meal to feel better about my situation. God uses these relationships to ease my mind, uplift my spirit, and remind me that I am not alone.

In times of uncertainty or change, isolation can creep in, which makes it so easy to throw a pity party. Trust me, I know. You may want to become detached, stay down, or wallow in despair. Just realize, the enemy uses isolation as a tactic to keep you down. God, on the other hand, does not want you to stay in isolation. He wants you to connect with others as a source of support.

You are an overcomer in Christ Jesus. If you don't have family or friends nearby, be creative in finding ways to stay connected. A small local group or a trusted online community made up of people who have had similar life experiences is essential in helping you form a circle of invaluable support.

As a first-time mom, I found incredible support from a local moms group where I shared my joys and challenges of raising a newborn. Listening to similar stories from other moms reminded me that I am not alone and helped to calm many of my anxieties.

Don't let isolation or depression have the final say. God created us to be in community and form strong, Godly relationships for encouragement and support. With each new day and mercy, seek community and relationships that will uplift and strengthen your spirit.

Prayer

Dear God, thank You for the community You have provided me, to uplift me. In times when I am isolated and feel down, may You comfort and strengthen me. In Jesus' name, amen.

Action

Who will you reach out to, to form and maintain your community of support? Name a person or group that will provide encouragement for you during this season.

Don't let isolation or depression have the final say. God created us to be in community and form strong, Godly relationships for encouragement and support.

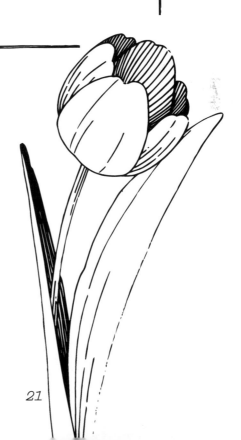

But godliness with contentment is great gain. For we brought nothing into the world, and we can take nothing out of it.

I Timothy 6:6–7

Comparison will Steal Contentment

Social media is a powerful networking tool, but it is also a comparison trap. Scrolling through endless photos of seemingly flawless people and their seemingly perfect lives can leave you feeling inadequate and drained, but you keep wanting to see more. I have often compared my ministry, season, or life to other women. The ones I pay attention to the most are those who have larger ministries than mine or more followers.

It's okay to aspire and ask yourself, "What do I need to do more of?" But comparing your life or purpose to another person's is at best counter-productive and at worst dangerous if it breeds jealousy, discontent, and division. Comparison can steal your joy and peace. It also distracts you from what God has called you to do. God has called you for a unique purpose, so continue to walk in that purpose with assurance, focus, and boldness.

It's worth repeating:
- Comparison will steal your joy.
- Comparison will steal your peace.
- Comparison will leave you continually frustrated and wanting "more."
- Comparison will keep you envious.
- Comparison will shift your focus from God's blessings to what "they" have.
- Comparison will have you feeling stuck and insecure instead of moving forward with confidence.

When you find yourself comparing your life to the next person, pray to God for guidance to free you. I invite you to receive God's contentment today. Celebrate and give God thanks for the ways in which He is using you and your gifts.

Prayer

Dear God, thank You for the purpose You have called me to and the unique gifts You have given me to accomplish it. I surrender my temptation towards comparison. Help me to be content and focus on the path You have chosen for me.

In Jesus' name, amen

Action

List all the ways you compare yourself to others on social media. Which area or areas of comparison can you pray about and surrender to God for His guidance and redemption?

When you find yourself comparing your life to the next person, pray to God for guidance to free you.

I can do everything through him who gives me strength.

Philippians 4:13

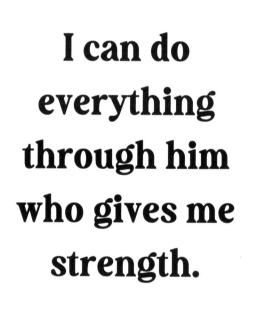

You are Stronger Than You Feel

Our feelings are fleeting. To be honest, my feelings fluctuate from minute to minute. I can be energized in the morning and tired by midday. Some days I feel I can accomplish all that is before me, and then other days I feel deficient. Sound familiar? Still, you can't allow your feelings to lead you. Instead, be led by God's Word and Spirit in the direction He wants you to go. God wants your decisions and actions to be Holy Spirit-led and not emotions-led.

The wonderful news about God is that because He created us, and because of His omniscience, He knows every reaction, every emotion, and every attitude you will ever have, and He wants you to depend on Him more for tenacity, endurance, peace, and instruction. The times when I allow my feelings to dominate my mind and overtake me are the times when I'm trying to "fix" everything, solve a problem, or just handle it by myself. When I allow my feelings to address my circumstances instead of God, I often feel worse because I'm left frustrated, overwhelmed, and more burdened. However, when I step aside by faith and make room for God to fight my battles, my mind is at ease and I am at peace as I take action in the way He directs and guides me.

Giving in to your emotions is counter-productive. Emotion-led actions tend to lead you to more problems ultimately, even to a point where you want to quit while God wants you to move forward. But know that, with Christ, you are stronger than you *feel*. God offers you stability when you focus your thoughts, decision-making, and actions on Him. His strength is made perfect in your weakness, and that is why you are more than a conqueror through Him. Jesus Christ is the One who sustains you for the journey. Allow Him to fortify you and surrender your feelings to Him. Be anchored in Christ.

Prayer

Dear God, thank You for being the source of my strength. Forgive me for times when I have allowed my feelings to lead me, and not Your Word. I lean on Your Spirit for help and for all that I need to move forward.

In Jesus' name, amen.

Action

Write down three to five feelings that you've been experiencing in this current season. For each feeling, find a scripture to uplift and encourage you.

*With Christ, you are
stronger than you feel.*

'Take my yoke
upon you and
learn from me, for
I am gentle and
humble in heart,
and you will find
rest for your
souls.'

Matthew 11:29

An Empty Vessel Must Be Filled

You know you need to slow down, but you keep going at a high speed and stopping only to eat and sleep . . . barely. Your body and mind are telling you to rest. You know you've been running on empty for far too long. But you ignore the physical signs and the irritability because there's just so much that needs to get done and you believe you're the only one who can do it. You're not alone. Life these days is filled with so much work to do, errands to run, and challenges to face, that the thought of rest makes us think we don't want to waste the time. So, running on empty is the new norm. But God can't use you as fully or effectively if you're working from a depleted tank. In order for you to be the person God calls you to be, you need to be a good steward of your temple. Part of being a good steward is recharging and being filled up with proper self-care. Like a car that runs on gas, you must continually be refueled with God's Word and His Spirit so that you can run the race He has set before you. An empty vessel must be filled so that it can move forward and get to its destination with purpose, power, and courage.You cannot give to and serve others with what is not being regularly filled up within yourself. If you've been serving on "empty" for far too long, today I invite you to recommit to being filled with the only thing that can refresh your soul: God's Word, the Holy Bible.

- Be filled with the energizing and inspiring power of the Scriptures and the Holy Spirit.
- Be filled with vigor for your burdened soul, so that you can serve from a place of overflowing joy.
- Be filled with the knowledge that God is the ultimate source of your strength to keep going.
- Be filled with God's Word to encourage, empower, and equip you as you live out your purpose and share His lovingkindness with others.
- Be filled to recharge your body, mind, and spirit.

Prayer

Dear God, thank You for renewing my mind, body, and spirit with Your Word and direction for my life. Please forgive me when I have allowed other things or relationships to distract me from focusing on You. Thank You for providing me with the wisdom to know when rest is needed. In Jesus' name, amen.

Action

Name one specific way that you will be intentional about being filled with the things of God. What is one habit that you will put down that is draining you?

*You cannot give to and
serve others with what is
not being regularly
filled up within yourself.*

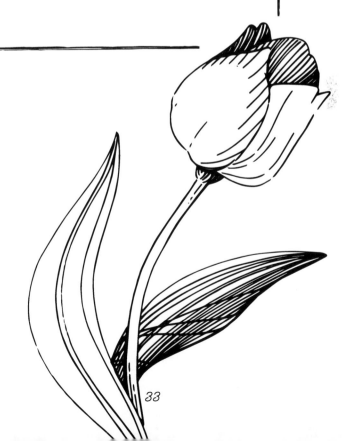

'Come with me by yourselves to a quiet place and get some rest.'

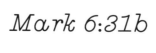

Mark 6:31b

Unplug

Living in a tech savvy world, we are consumed with social media. Being on our phones keeps many of us from being fully "present" in the moment, especially when it comes to spending quality time with those who matter most to us. Often, when I wake up in the morning, I pick up my phone before doing anything else, including spending time with God. Yes, I said it! Before my devotional time, I've placed my "need" to scroll social media first so that I don't miss anything. While God has convicted me multiple times about unplugging from my phone, that nagging "need to know" always seems to draw me back in.

While scrolling social media may fill a temporary void, such as perhaps the need for connection, absolutely nothing can replace growing in your relationship with God. I invite you to join me and regularly unplug from technology for a while and plug instead into a real presence and real conversations with people closest to you. Unplug from social media and connect with family and close friends by calling them on the phone or going out to lunch with them.

- Unplug to put God first.
- Unplug to drown out the noise of comparison and envy that plague social media circles.
- Unplug to limit distractions so that you can focus on being more present with family and other relationships that give life to your spirit.
- Unplug to remind yourself that your ultimate source for affirmation, assurance, and faith is God alone.

If you've been struggling with unplugging, I encourage you to pray to God for the courage and boldness to reaffirm your commitment to Him by focusing on what truly matters: cultivating a stronger relationship with Christ.

Prayer

Dear God, thank You for helping me unplug and drown out the noise that comes with allowing social media to consume me. Help me to find contentment in You alone and to spend more quality time nurturing relationships with people in my life who truly matter. In Jesus' name, amen.

Action

How can you unplug? What specific actions will you take to replace that time so that you can spend more time with a person who matters?

*Unplug to remind
yourself that your
ultimate source for
affirmation, assurance,
and faith is God alone.*

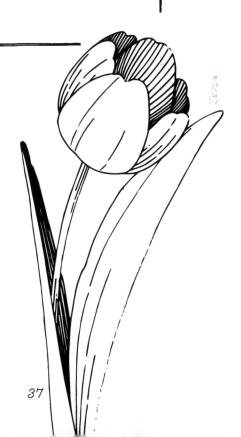

Now faith is confidence in what we hope for and assurance about what we do not see.

Hebrews 11:1

Move Forward in Faith

You will never have all the answers, but God wants you to move forward in faith. When God calls you to a specific place, assignment, or purpose, move forward in faith and trust that He will direct your path. In times of uncertainty, fear, or trial, God is reminding you that He will never leave you or forsake you.

When making a decision, many times I over-analyze the situation or my options to the point that I end up not doing anything. I'm too busy trying to predict and work out all the possible outcomes. If you try to control everything and move ahead of God, you are not fully depending on Him. The result is that often you miss out on His great plans for you! Wanting to control every area of your life will leave you overwhelmed, drained, and not leaving room for God to enter in and move on your behalf.

God speaks this truth: You are not in control, and you must surrender. Trust His guidance. God wants to strengthen your faith by showing you His way for moving forward.

Move forward in faith even when you don't know the way.

Move forward in faith even when doubt, fear, and anxiety set in.

Move forward in faith to experience God's continued faithfulness and great plans for your life.

Move forward in faith even though the outcome may be out of your control.

Move forward in faith to be reminded that God will safely lead you and has an amazing plan for your life.

Prayer

Dear God, thank You for being faithful to me at all times. As I move forward in life, please increase my faith in You and the plans You have for my life. In times when I don't believe, please help my unbelief. In Jesus' name, amen.

Action

Write about a specific experience in your life where you are seeking to move forward in faith.

God wants to strengthen your faith by showing you His way for moving forward.

Love is patient, love is kind.

I Corinthians 13:4a

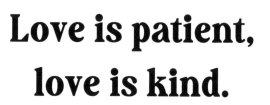

Be Kind to One Another

Jesus instructs us to be kind to one another, but showing kindness sometimes requires us to step out of our comfort zone and be selfless. In a world of continual division and self-ambition, showing kindness is not always the top priority. It is so easy to be preoccupied with our daily routine and challenges that we neglect being kind to other people. Also, many times it seems that showing too much kindness is perceived as weakness. Despite that perception, God calls you to be kind anyway. Try not to withhold your kindness out of rejection, fear, or feelings of inadequacy. Look past your feelings and show kindness anyway. I invite you to show a small act of kindness every day to a person you come in contact with.

In addition, continue to show kindness to yourself. Be kind to yourself by encouraging and empowering your spirit during difficult seasons. I'm often my harshest critic, wanting to have everything go smoothly and be flawless. However, perfection is impossible. You have to be kind to yourself, remembering that God is with you even during every mistake and mishap. Here are some simple and practical ways you can show kindness each day:

- Be kind by holding the door open for someone, and saying hello and thank you.
- Be kind by encouraging someone with an uplifting word, a listening ear, or an affirming scripture.
- Be kind by representing the light and love of Christ to others.
- Be kind by encouraging, empowering, and reassuring yourself when you want to quit.

Let God's love and kindness permeate your being. Share that kindness with other people. Don't forget to be kind and show grace to yourself every day, too.

Prayer

Dear God, thank You for the loving kindness You show to me every day. Give me the courage and desire to show kindness to my family, friends, and those I interact with daily, as I continue to represent Your Light.

In Jesus' name, amen.

Action

Name at least two or three things you can do each day to show kindness to others and yourself.

Be kind to yourself,
remembering that God
is with you even during
every mistake and
mishap.

And my God will meet all your needs according to the riches of his glory in Christ Jesus.

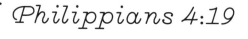

Philippians 4:19

God Will Supply All of Your Needs

God said He will supply all of your needs, not all of your wants. There is a difference. Too often, I have spent so much time focusing on what I think I don't have, instead of celebrating all the needs God has met and continues to meet for me. For example, there were times when money was tight, but all my bills were paid. When I needed volunteers for my mentoring program, God provided. When I was seeking peace, renewal, restoration, or healing, God showed up. During each season of my life when I didn't see a way, God made a way out of no way.

When God calls you for a distinct purpose and assignment, He will equip you with all that you need to fulfill your calling. Things may be difficult and there will be seasons where you don't understand the road ahead, but remain encouraged that God is still always with you and for you.

Today, I invite you to take a pause and write down and give thanks to God for every need He has met for you. Ask yourself, "How are my immediate needs being met?" Pray for God's guidance, wisdom, and patience when you are frustrated. Renew your mind and shift your focus away from what you don't have. Give God praise for His abundant blessings.

- God supplies all your needs, because He has great love for you and He cares about you.
- God supplies all your needs, to equip you to accomplish the assignments He has given to you.
- God supplies all your needs because He promises in His Word that He will never leave you or forsake you.

Prayer

Dear God, thank You for providing all my needs to accomplish Your will. In times when I doubt and focus on what I don't have, remind me of the many ways you continue to provide.
In Jesus' name, amen.

Action

In your devotional time, take time to write down between five and ten needs that God has met recently. Then, openly praise Him and thank Him as an act of worship.

When God calls you for a
distinct purpose and
assignment, He will
equip you with all that
you need to fulfill your
calling.

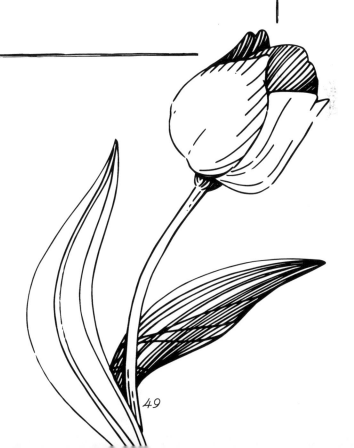

We have different gifts, according to the grace given to each of us...

Romans 12:6a

Use Your Gifts

How many times have you not used a gift or gift card someone has given you? It sits, collects dust, and a person's hard earned money goes to waste. Similar to an unused physical gift, God blesses you with unique spiritual gifts that are designed to empower, uplift, and encourage others. There may be many reasons why you don't use any or all of your God-given gifts. You may be afraid, uncertain, or unsure of where to start.

Today, I invite you to use the gifts you have been given for God's glory. If you are seeking direction and wisdom on what your gifts are, how to use them, and where to start, pray for God to counsel you.

We are all given unique gifts and abilities that are designed for a specific purpose as part of representing God's Light and love. Don't lose hope. Know that your gifts will make room for you. The enemy would love nothing more than for you to keep your gifts hidden, laying dormant and unused. The exciting news is that your gifts do not have an expiration date and will ultimately be used to achieve God's purpose in your life.

- Use your gifts to represent God's glory.
- Use your gifts to reassure, uplift, and provide hope for someone else.
- Use your gifts to live out your God-given purpose.
- Use your gifts to be a living witness to the body of Christ.
- Use your gifts to be the leader that God has called you to be.

Prayer

Dear God, thank You for the specific gifts You have given me to use for Your glory and to serve others. Grant me the fortitude and courage to use them with boldness and zeal. When I am unsure about what my gifts are or how to use them, thank You for giving me wisdom through Your Word and prayer. In Jesus' name, amen.

Action

Name one specific gift that God is calling you to use and share with others to represent His glory. Write it down and pray for guidance on how you will use it, and when.

Use the gifts you have been given for God's glory.

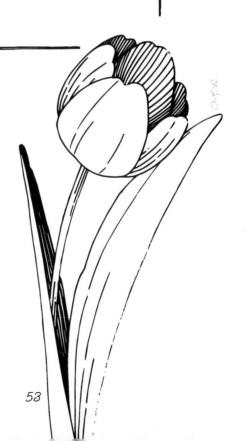

Do not be anxious about anything, but in every situation, by prayer and petition with thanksgiving, present your requests to God. And the peace of God, which transcends all understanding, will guard your hearts and your minds in Christ Jesus.

Philippians 4:6-7

Receive God's Peace

God's peace is available to you. Say it aloud: "I receive God's peace today." This daily affirmation is essential for you to not only say, but fully believe.

I have learned that receiving peace doesn't mean there is no struggle. God's peace will cover and keep you even in the midst of life's challenges.

When I have felt anxious or overwhelmed from a situation or challenge before me, God's peace has uplifted me and shifted my perspective. My circumstance may not immediately change, but my outlook and response will.

You can choose. Receive God's peace, or live in constant anxiety.

- God's peace will calm you when you are frantic.
- God's peace will direct you when you feel lost.
- God's peace will encourage you when you want to quit.
- God's peace will strengthen you when you feel weak.

I invite you to receive God's peace today.

Prayer

Dear God, thank You for Your peace that is available to me when I am anxious. Help me to receive Your peace, to comfort and calm my troubled mind.
In Jesus' name, amen.

Action

Look in a mirror and say, "Lord, I receive your peace today." Say it as many times as you need to in order to get it down in your spirit for encouragement. Record it, too, and play it during different moments of your day, as a regular reminder.

God's peace will cover
and keep you even in the
midst of life's
challenges.

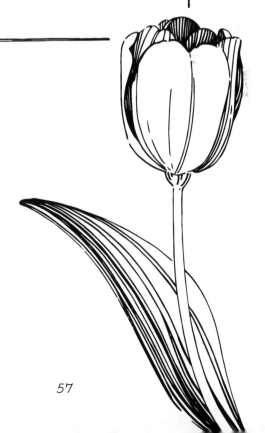

I lift up my eyes to
the hills—where
does my help
come from?
My help comes
from the LORD,
the Maker of
heaven and earth.

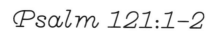

Psalm 121:1–2

Start With A Single Step

While you are waiting for the ideal conditions or to have all your "ducks in a row," which may never come, you can start with a single step. God has been speaking to you and has given you a vision and an assignment to accomplish, but you've been analyzing and coming up with all the reasons you think it won't work or all the things you think you don't have. Yet, God will prepare and provide for every vision He has given you.

Start with one step. Write a paragraph for a book. Walk for exercise. Don't allow paralysis of analysis to set in. God will permit you to move forward and grant you everything you need.

Surrender your fears and anxieties to Him. Allow the Holy Spirit to fill you with courage, boldness, and the desire to want to move forward.

When you get out of your own mind and relinquish your control over to God's will, you are able to propel forward with greater confidence and faith, knowing that it is God who is leading you. Leave the distractions of perfectionism and self-doubt at the feet of Jesus.

Newsflash: You will never have all the answers or fully understand the hows and whys of your life. Focus instead on trusting God more with the details and have the courage to say "yes" when He calls you.

Today, I invite you to take one single step forward. God is for you and is cheering you on!

Prayer

Dear God, thank You for giving me the courage and boldness to move forward in faith with the gifts, dreams, and visions You have given me. When I am hesitant or have fear, thank You for Your peace that calms and empowers me to take one single step forward. In Jesus' name, amen.

Action

Write down one specific action you will take for a goal you have during this season. What single step will you take to help you progress forward towards a goal?

Allow the Holy Spirit to fill you with courage, boldness, and the desire to want to move forward.

Cast all your anxiety on him because he cares for you.

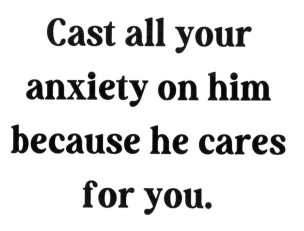

1 Peter 5:7

Cast Your Cares to God

When I am tired, stressed, or feeling overwhelmed, it shows. Oftentimes, my outward countenance and demeanor look weighed down. The worries of my mind manifest in my spirit. I'm trying to carry it all and manage it all.

Sound familiar? You may be in a season where you feel weighed down from the exhaustion of trying to keep it all together. Free yourself of the daunting task of having to be all things to all people. Trying to keep it all together takes a toll and doesn't allow much room for God to get the right kind of attention in our hearts and lives.

Friend, there is good news today: God is calling you to cast all your cares to Him. Casting your cares is not a simple catchphrase, but a daily, practiced spiritual discipline. When you cast your cares to the Lord, you are depending on Him to have complete control, acknowledging that you can't do everything by yourself. God wants you to be free from the burden of sin and fighting life's battles on your own.

Cast every care, anxiety, and weight you have to God. You will feel lighter, your mind will be renewed, and God will reassure you that you are not alone. God cares for you so much that He wants you to live in freedom. Be reassured today that God is for you and He lovingly desires for you to come to Him with all of your burdens.

- Cast your cares to God, so that your load will be lighter.
- Cast your cares to God, to be reminded that you are not alone.
- Cast your cares to God, and let God rejuvenate and preserve you during each season.

Prayer

Dear God, thank you that I can come to You at any time, and that You welcome all of my joys, cares, fears, and anxieties. When I want to carry the weight of the world on my shoulders, point out to me that You already did that for me. Thank You for helping me commit all my cares to You, and thank You that You will continue to cover me. In Jesus' name, amen.

Action

List every care you currently are facing in this season. Now, pick one specific thing or circumstance that you will cast over to God today. Take it to Him in prayer.

Cast every care, anxiety, and weight you have to God.

Finally, be strong in the LORD and in his mighty power.

Ephesians 6:10

Strengthen Your Spiritual Muscle

Lifting weights helps build the physical muscles in your body. Lifting even a small amount consistently over time will provide a strong foundation for developing definition and durability. But when you don't take the time to strengthen your physical body, discomfort and pain can set in.

Similarly, in order to strengthen your spiritual muscles, it is essential that you stay connected to God. You do that by reading and studying God's Word, praying diligently, and sharing the hope of eternal life in Christ with others. Keeping your spiritual muscles strengthened will help keep you determined and hopeful during life's challenges.

Sometimes when I feel overwhelmed and stretched beyond my capacity, that's when I choose to let my spiritual muscles feed and replenish me. Your spiritual muscles help to remind you to fully depend, trust, and rely on God to assist you. By your own power, you become exhausted and depleted of energy. Spiritual muscles become your source of renewal, restoration, and reassurance that God loves and cares for you.

- Strengthen your spiritual muscles, to help support you when life gets tough.
- Strengthen your spiritual muscles, to be encouraged with the renewing, affirming, and restorative power of God's Word.
- Strengthen your spiritual muscles, to be always mindful that you are not alone.
- Strengthen your spiritual muscles, so that you don't quit.

Prayer

Dear God, thank You for strengthening my spiritual muscles each day and giving me the desire and discipline to stay connected to You. When life is challenging, thank You for Your Word that boosts and brightens my spirit to press forward. In Jesus' name, amen.

Action

Name at least two or three specific ways that you can begin to strengthen your spiritual muscles.

Strengthen your spiritual muscles, to help support you when life gets tough.

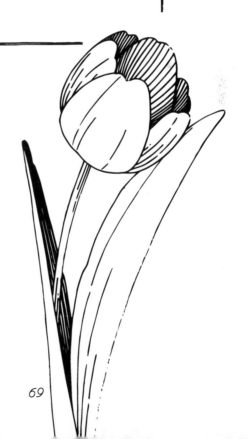

From him the whole body, joined and held together by every supporting ligament, grows and builds itself in love, as each part does its work.

Ephesians 4:16

Collaborate with Others

There is power in coming together and unifying as the Body of Christ. God has given each of us unique gifts and natural abilities, which we are to use to glorify Him and bless others. No person is an island, and God doesn't want us to do everything by ourselves.

Oftentimes, I've had the mindset that, "If I don't do it, it won't get done." Everything had to be done according to my specifications for it to be acceptable. But over time, God has shown me that the "I can do it all by myself" mindset is selfish. It does not make room for collaboration and for greater dependence on Him.

Conversely, when you unify with others to accomplish a God-given purpose, it is powerful and allows everyone to operate within his or her strengths. It's okay to ask for help. It's okay not to have control. It's okay not to be perfect. Collaborating is not a sign of weakness, but a sign of wisdom.

- Collaborate with others, to unify with the Body of Christ.
- Collaborate with others, to allow the gifts of others to shine.
- Collaborate with others, because no person is an island.
- Collaborate with others, to form deeper, more meaningful connections.
- Collaborate with others, to revitalize, lift up, and support them during both joyous and challenging seasons of life.

Today, I invite you to not carry the load by yourself. Collaborate with those whom God places in your path to uphold and re-energize you.

Prayer

Dear God, thank You that You have called me into community with others. Help me to see the support and resources You have placed around me, to accomplish Your will. Thank You for the divinely ordained connections that You have appointed. In Jesus' name, amen.

Action

Name and reach out to at least two people you will ask for assistance to support you during this season. Write down each name and the date you will reach out, to hold yourself accountable.

Collaborating is not a
sign of weakness, but a
sign of wisdom.

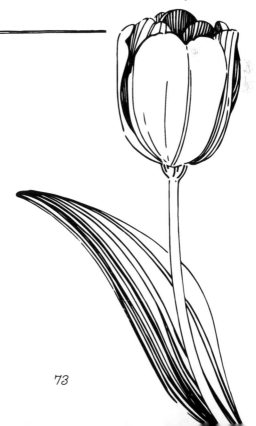

Do not grieve, for the joy of the LORD is your strength.

Nehemiah 8:10d

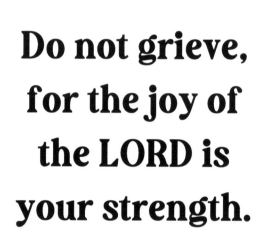

Find Your Joyful Place

Finding joy each day is not an emotion, but a decision. When you wake up each day, you may be faced with many situations and circumstances that attempt to steal your joy. For instance, a misunderstanding, a rude driver, an aggressive co-worker, an unruly child, or an abrupt change of your plans. I often find myself letting a minor occurrence rub me so much the wrong way that I remain upset about it for the rest of the day.

Sound familiar? Thankfully, God has shown me it's not healthy and fruitful to allow my emotions to dictate my state of mind and outlook. He desires for me to seek the joy of the Lord.

When your emotions consume you, you are allowing yourself to remain frustrated, exhausted, and generally not at peace. That's why finding your joyful place is a daily commitment, where you make a conscious decision to let God be your peace and anchor every day.

- Choose joy, to reinforce your spiritual muscle each day.
- Choose joy, so you won't allow your circumstances to overtake you.
- Choose joy to represent Christ's love and contentment in your soul.
- Choose joy to combat the negative thinking and self-doubt whenever it comes.
- Choose joy to claim victory over the schemes of the enemy.

Finding joy is not dependent on everything going right, but it is an assurance that God is near. If you've been allowing your emotions to consume you, I invite you to choose joy. Despite how challenging your circumstances may be, let the joy of the Lord fill you. God's joy will rejuvenate and restore you. Emotions are fleeting, but God's joy is steadfast.

Prayer

Dear God, thank You for Your joy, which is available to me and helps to combat my weariness. In those times when I focus on my circumstances instead of You, thank You for Your joy that restores me. In Jesus' name, amen.

Action

How will you be purposeful about finding your joyful place? Name some of God's attributes that remind you of His goodness and that can take you to your joyful place.

Finding joy is not dependent on everything going right, but it is an assurance that God is near.

If we confess our sins, He is faithful and just and will forgive us our sins and purify us from all unrighteousness.

1 John 1:9

Forgive Yourself

If Christ died on the cross for the forgiveness of our sins, why is it so hard for us to forgive ourselves? Life is not a perfect line from A to Z. Many changes, interruptions, and detours pop up along the way. We all have sinned and fallen short of the glory of God. When I make a mistake, I am usually my harshest critic. Over the years, I have beaten myself up for my mistakes and over-analyzed what I could have done differently. Remember, though, that mistakes will happen, but also remember that God's grace is greater. During the moments when you fall short, God wants you to depend on Him all the more. Don't retreat away from Him but come even closer to Him, with a humble heart. He desires to show you that He is your loving Father who can help you change.

Due to His great love for you, God teaches, shepherds, and directs you with loving kindness, patience, and grace. In order to move forward and trust that God is in control, it is important to forgive yourself first. Each new day provides a new opportunity for you to start again, having learned from the lessons of yesterday. Celebrate what is going well, and give yourself permission to not have it "all" together. This transformed way of thinking will help free you from the bondage of your past mistakes.

- Forgive yourself, and walk in freedom.
- Forgive yourself, and forgive others.
- Forgive yourself, and receive the beautiful gift of God's grace.
- Forgive yourself, because no one is perfect.
- Forgive yourself and embrace the lessons you learned.
- Forgive yourself so that generational strongholds will be broken.
- Forgive yourself, because Jesus already forgave you when He died on the cross for your sins.

Prayer

Dear God, thank You for sending Your Son Jesus to die on the cross and redeem me of my sins. Please help me to forgive myself for my own imperfections. Extend grace to me so that I can walk in full freedom that You have made available to me. In Jesus' name, amen.

Action

Write down five mistakes you have made in your past. How can you forgive yourself and learn from those mistakes so that you can be more free to receive God's grace daily?

> *Celebrate what is going well, and give yourself permission to not have it "all" together.*

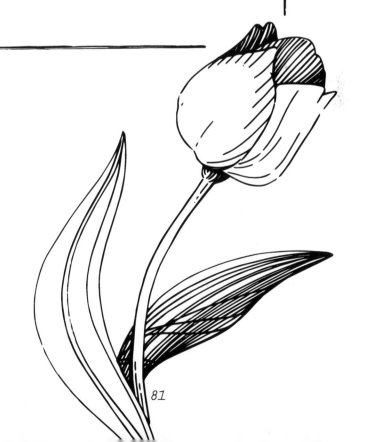

The prayer of a righteous person is powerful and effective.

James 5:16c

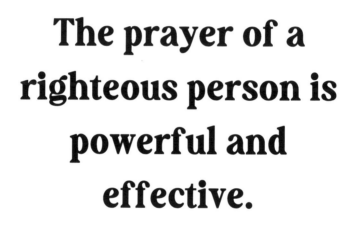

Pray Without Ceasing

Prayer is powerful! When I pray, I am able to talk to God freely and without pretense. Through prayer, God has healed my body, calmed my fears, revitalized my spirit, and restored strained relationships. I know prayer works. Prayer is a powerful tool to stay connected to God and to overcome the lies of the enemy. Your prayers and the expression of them don't have to be limited to a church building or a specific time of day. God wants you to come before Him just as you are, with every care, fear, anxiety, and joy surrendered to Him. When you pray to God consistently, your relationship with Him and your desire to confide in Him as your closest friend and confidant strengthens.

Ultimately, prayer is personal. It provides you with an opportunity to come boldly and confidently to your Heavenly Father with your praises, requests, fears, and anxieties, and to seek Him for wisdom and direction. God doesn't want pretense, the perfect words, or a rehearsed script. God desires for you to simply come.

You can pray and talk to God just as you are, with a bruised ego, a broken spirit, insecurities, joys, fears, and uncertainties. That is amazing news! Prayer is an open invitation for you to talk with your caring Father and Friend!

- Pray without ceasing, and be transformed.
- Pray without ceasing, to be set free.
- Pray without ceasing, because prayer is a weapon to overcome the enemy.
- Pray without ceasing, and be healed to walk forward with boldness.
- Pray without ceasing, and listen for wisdom and direction as you sit in God's presence.
- Don't focus on how you pray, but continue to cultivate a daily spiritual discipline of prayer.

Prayer

Dear God, thank You for the gift of prayer that You have made available to me. Thank You that I can come to You just as I am, to talk to you, and You listen to me and give me wisdom. Thank You for moving in ways seen and unseen. In Jesus' name, amen.

Action

How will you be intentional about praying each day? Write it down as a guide.

Prayer is a powerful tool to stay connected to God and to overcome the lies of the enemy.

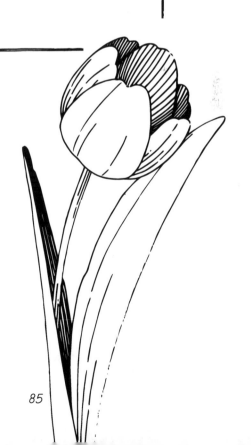

Be still,
and know
I am God...

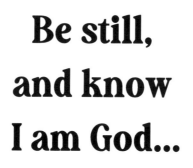

Psalm 46:10a

Be Still for a Season

Serving God and being still in God's presence are two different things. It is so easy to become so preoccupied with "doing" ministry or other work that we neglect being still in God's presence. We live in a fast-paced society that has conditioned us to expect instant results.

Being still doesn't mean you do nothing. It means that you slow down long enough to sit in God's presence and let Him speak to you. When you are still, you acknowledge that God is the source of your vitality and that therefore you need to surrender your will to His will every day.

Busyness has become synonymous with success. However, God calls you to be still for a season. When you are still, God is able to guide your next steps in your journey. I am most filled when I slow down and sit in God's presence. God renews my mind and realigns my focus.

Being still doesn't mean that you are completely quiet or that you cease from doing anything. While being still has an added benefit of slowing down, it is also more of developing a mindset and posture of greater dependence on God.

- Be still, to hear more clearly from God.
- Be still, to trust and depend on God more.
- Be still, to drown out the distractions.
- Be still, to be recharged and renewed.
- Be still, to be reminded that God is in control.

Prayer

Dear God, thank You for helping me to be still and trust You more. In the stillness, may my relationship with You grow stronger, and may I listen to You to gain more clarity, wisdom, and direction for my life. In Jesus' name, amen.

Action

How will you embrace being still in this season?

Be still, to hear more clearly from God.

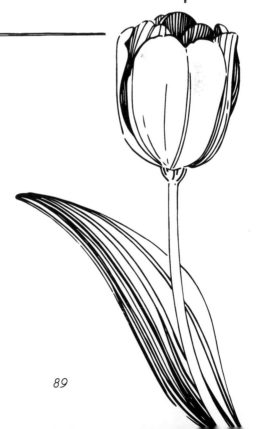

Above all else, guard your heart, for everything you do flows from it.

Proverbs 4:23

Guard Your Heart

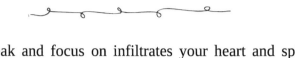

What you speak and focus on infiltrates your heart and spirit. Make every effort to guard your heart by what you think, listen to, and let consume your mind. While the world focuses on outward appearances, each day your heart is on full display before God.

Your heart guides your thoughts, actions, and attitudes each moment of the day, and God has a firsthand view into what lies deep within you, beneath the surface. As you draw closer to Him, sharing every aspect of your heart and brokenness to Him, He will mend your broken pieces. When you speak negative self-talk, or have anxieties that attempt to steal your joy, immediately ask God to cleanse and renew your heart so that you can start fresh. The good news is that God cares about you.

He loves you so much that the condition of your heart is His top priority.

Your heart reveals your true and authentic self.
Your heart reveals the deeper, most meaningful issues.
God is concerned most with the matters of your heart, and there is no pretense, facade, or ill motives that He can't see. So, guard your heart and allow God to turn what has been broken into wholeness.

Today, I invite you to guard your heart and allow God to invigorate, heal, and restore the pieces that are hurting, and you will be made whole.

Prayer

Dear God, thank You for helping me guard my heart as I invite You in to uplift me. Forgive me for times when I have allowed negative thoughts, attitudes, or behaviors consume my heart. Thank You for loving me anew each day. In Jesus' name, amen.

Action

Write down the areas of your heart that are broken, then surrender them over to God. What specific steps will you take to guard your heart more?

_____

_____

_____

_____

_____

_____

Guard your heart and allow God to turn what has been broken into wholeness.

My dear brothers
and sisters, take
note of this:
Everyone should
be quick to listen,
slow to speak and
slow to become
angry.

James 1:19

Talk Less, Listen More

There is nothing like a good conversation with a family member or friend you haven't talked to in a while. Catching up with a good friend refreshes me and I'm excited about our time together. During those times, it's important to listen intently and not do all the talking. Talking without listening is problematic because it limits the value of the other person's experience in the conversation.

When I spend time with God, I often do a lot of talking. That is, I have prayer requests and speak what is on my heart. But, while sharing my heart with God, I have learned that there is also incredible power in listening to Him.

One of the best decisions you can make is to slow down your busy days, agendas, and to-do-lists to listen to God, who holds infinite wisdom and guidance for you. Today, I invite you to begin listening more to God and allowing the Holy Spirit to speak to you.

Be still and listen to what God is speaking to you. Drown out the distractions and listen. Strengthen your relationships by listening more. Listen, not always to have a response but to gain wisdom and understanding from another person's story.

- Listen to God's voice, so that you can be filled.
- Listen, to be directed.
- Listen, to be centered.
- Listen, to be led.
- Listen, to better serve others.

Prayer

Dear God, thank You for helping me listen to You more, gaining wisdom and guidance for my life. Help me to listen to others, to gain understanding and be a loving friend or family member. Thank You for speaking to me and leading me. In Jesus' name, amen.

Action

How can you actively listen more to God and to others in your life?

Listen to God's voice, so that you can be filled.

Love never fails. And now these three remain: faith, hope and love. But the greatest of these is love.

1 Corinthians 13:8,13

Let Love Lead

Love is a powerful trait that Jesus modeled and that we strive to follow each day. God loves us so much that He gave us His only Son to die for us. (John 3:16) God's love is unconditional and is always the motivation for His interactions with us. That is great news!

During difficult seasons and navigating challenging relationships, allow yourself to be filled with God's love. You will be strengthened and encouraged as He guides you. God's love always covers you and draws you either back into or deeper into a relationship with Him.

Human love is fleeting, but God's love runs deep and is consistent and reliable. Even when you don't feel like loving, God's Spirit will empower you to walk in love anyway.

- Love is not a feeling but a decision; it is not dependent on feelings.
- Love is what should lead your motives and actions.
- Love unites, it does not divide.
- Love heals, unifies, and comforts.
- Loving those who show you love in return is easy. But loving those who are difficult and different is the true test and sign of spiritual maturity.

Prayer

Dear God, thank You for loving me unconditionally. Thank You for empowering me to represent You and to lead with love with my family, friends, and others I interact with on a daily basis. In times when I am not able to love, please direct me.
In Jesus' name, amen.

Action

Who can you love better today? Name one or two people whom God is calling you to love better, and pray for His guidance on what specific steps to take.

*During difficult seasons,
allow yourself to be filled
with God's love.*

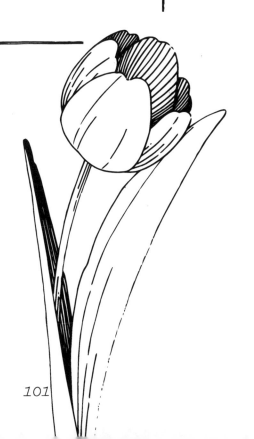

Create in me a pure heart, O God, and renew a steadfast spirit within me.

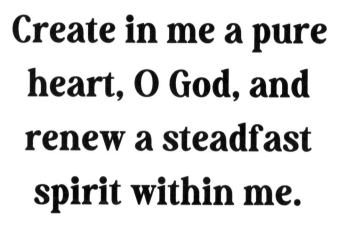

Psalm 51:10

Serve with Compassion

I have a heart for serving others. Over the last 20 years, God has used me to serve in ministry with children, youth, and women, and I have been blessed to see Him move in the hearts of His people and transform their lives through me. It is so fulfilling to listen, support, and encourage others with the hope and love of Jesus Christ.

Serving with compassion allows you to actively engage and empathize with those you are entrusted to serve. Continually examine your motives and spirit, to ensure that you are serving and leading from a place of compassion and not obligation nor selfish ambition.

Despite whatever your personal challenges may be, God is calling you to walk alongside another person and share the love of Christ. Show compassion by actively listening, encouraging, and providing practical wisdom and resources. We don't need to have all the answers; the ministry of presence is just as powerful.

- Serve with compassion, to encourage, uplift, and empower someone else.
- Serve with compassion, by being present, walking alongside someone, and listening in their time of need.
- Serve with compassion, to represent God's love and heart.

Prayer

Dear God, thank You for placing in me a heart and spirit full of compassion while I'm serving. Thank You for instilling in me the desire to be present in other people's lives, uplifting and encouraging them. Give me the eyes to see whom You would want me to minister to with compassion.

In Jesus' name, amen.

Action

Think about how God is calling you to show compassion while serving. What are some ways that compassion can be shown?

Serving with compassion allows you to actively engage and empathize with those you are entrusted to serve.

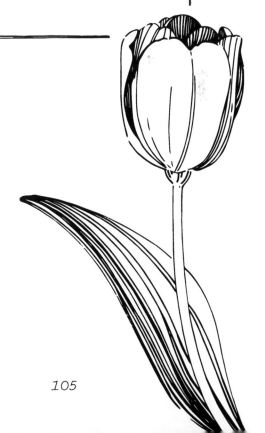

Do not conform to the pattern of this world, but be transformed by the renewing of your mind. Then you will be able to test and approve what God's will is--his good, pleasing and perfect will.

Romans 12:2

Renew Your Mind Daily

Our thoughts have the power to build up or tear down. When I allow my thoughts to wander, then fear, insecurity, envy, and anxiety set in. Many times, I have thoughts and create scenarios that are untrue and completely contrary to God's Word.

God can renew your mind with what He has written in the Holy Scriptures because His words help you combat negative thoughts. A renewed mind revolutionizes your focus and changes the trajectory of your life.

Today, I encourage you to realign your thoughts and renew your mind to speak life and hope over your present circumstances.

- Renew your mind, to be free from negative thinking.
- Renew your mind, to move forward in your God-given purpose.
- Renew your mind, to stay connected to God's Holy Word.
- Renew your mind, to overcome the schemes of the enemy.
- Renew your mind, to be equipped and empowered to pursue your purpose with boldness.

Prayer

Dear God, thank You for renewing my mind daily with Your Word, Your wisdom, and Your strength. In times when I allow my mind to be filled with thoughts that are contrary to what You say, please forgive me. Thank You for helping me to realign my mind, my thoughts, and my focus to You. In Jesus' name, amen.

Action

What specific practices will you commit to, to renew your mind?

A renewed mind
revolutionizes your focus
and changes the
trajectory of your life.

'For I know the plans
I have for you,'
declares the LORD,
'plans to prosper you
and not to harm you,
plans to give you
hope and a future.'

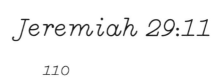

Jeremiah 29:11

Expect Greatness

In the above verse, God reminds Jeremiah that His plans for him are great. God has amazing plans for you, too, but you must first believe. God's plans don't happen according to your preconceived timeline, but according to His perfect will and timing.

As you continue to trust God and surrender control, His beautiful plan for you will unfold. He will equip, empower, and guide you, and as He does so, He will give you the courage and boldness to move forward in faith. You can expect greatness because of God's ultimate sovereignty. His plans for greatness in your life will not manifest within an isolated vacuum but within a community of support, encouragement, and resources.

- Expect greatness, to do mighty things as you yield to God's plans for you.
- Expect greatness, to break strongholds that God will equip you to overcome.
- Expect greatness, to be all that God has created you to be, because He will make it possible.
- Expect greatness, to live out your God-given identity, because you are beautifully and wonderfully made.

In order to continue to walk in greatness, you have to speak life and positive affirmation in your spirit. Recite different verses and passages from the Word of God, to help you combat negative self-talk and the lies of the enemy.

Believing in your greatness is essential to fully living out your God-given purpose, and you can encourage others to do the same.

Prayer

Dear God, thank You for the great plans that You have ordained for my life and the various ways You are moving on my behalf. Help me to continue to celebrate my abundant blessings and to move forward with boldness.

In Jesus' name, amen.

Action

How will you be great today?

Expect greatness, to do mighty things as you yield to God's plans for you.

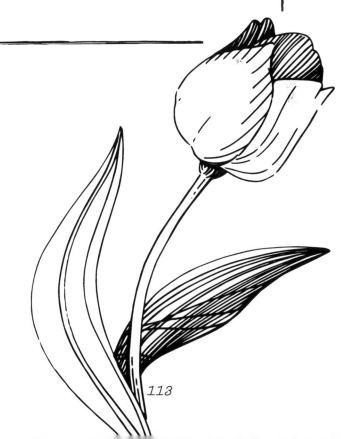

'For if you remain silent at this time, relief and deliverance for the Jews will arise from another place, but you and your father's family will perish.
And who knows but that you have come to your royal position for such a time as this?'

Esther 4:14

Find Your Voice

God has given you a unique voice, and the world needs to hear your testimony. But if you're like me, oftentimes you hold back from sharing your story with others because you're afraid of judgement, rejection, or shame about your past.

God will give you the courage you need to share your unique testimony about His faithfulness, so that you can boldly and with conviction serve as an encouragement and witness for His glory.

The enemy would want to try and silence your voice, to have you not share the Good News of Christ with others through your testimony. But, God has not given you a spirit of fear, but of power, love, and a sound mind.

- Find your voice, to share your testimony with others.
- Find your voice, to speak up for the oppressed and stand up against injustices.
- Find your voice, to speak God's Word and His promises over your life.
- Find your voice, to remind others that they are not alone.
- Find your voice, to speak of God's goodness.

How will you find your voice today?

Prayer

Dear God, thank You for providing me with a unique voice and giving me the courage and boldness to speak with clarity, courage, and conviction so that others are ministered to and You are glorified. In Jesus' name, amen.

Action

How will you use your voice to further fulfill God's purposes?

*Find your voice, to share
your testimony with
others.*

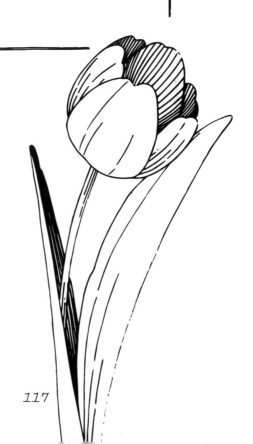

Journal

Journal

Journal

Journal

_____

_____

_____

_____

_____

_____

_____

_____

_____

_____

_____

_____

_____

_____

_____

_____

_____

_____

_____

_____

_____

Acknowledgements

First, I want to give thanks and praise to God who gave me the vision, guidance, wisdom, and inspiration to write this devotional. Without God's presence leading and directing me, this would not have happened. Praise God!

Thank you for the wonderful support, encouragement, and love of my husband, John and daughter, Naomi. You being in my corner means everything!

Thank you to my parents, brother, family, church family, and friends who continuously uplift, support and pray for me. You are simply the best!

Thank you to Laurel Davis of Empathy Editorial for your detailed and professional editing of this devotional. I truly appreciate all that you poured out to ensure the best final work possible.

Thank you to Jenny Erlingsson of Milk and Honey Books, who made my dream of publishing this devotional a reality. I appreciate your labor, creativity, listening ear, and resources you shared to help me cross the finish line!

About Author

Kirstyn Mayden is a Christian blogger who writes devotionals that empower and equip believers in their everyday lives. She is a wife, Mom, Pastor's wife, writer, speaker, non-profit leader and most importantly, loves Jesus with all her heart. She has a Master of Divinity degree from Emory University in Atlanta, GA. For the last 20 years, Kirstyn has served in several ministry capacities serving with children, youth, and women. She is also a contributing writer for Beloved Women, Bible Study Tools, and iBelieve.com.

She has a passion to serve with women empowering them to grow and live out their God-given purpose. Currently, she serves alongside her husband in ministry in West Virginia. She is a proud member of Delta Sigma Theta Sorority, Inc. In her free time, she enjoys reading, traveling, and spending time with family and friends.

Learn more at: www.kirstynspeakshope.com

Ministry Info

To stay updated on any future ministry projects with Kirstyn, you can connect with her on the following platforms:

- www.kirstynspeakshope.com

- Instagram: @kirstynsmayden

- Pinterest: www.pinterest.com/kirstynsmayden

- E-mail: kirstyn@kirstynspeakshope.com

Made in the USA
Columbia, SC
18 December 2023

28866460R00070